CONTENTS

PREFACE

This is an entrepreneurial constitution. Everything that is, has and will ever be is based in this book. We take apart the needle in a hay stack mentality and debunk it. A haystack is simply a pile of grass; the quickest way to remove a needle there in is by using a magnet. Period!

"It's just business and it's nothing personal", that's complete nonsense; the reason we go in to business is so that we can make money and eat. How is that not personal? We are not machines, we are humans, and this is precisely why there needs to exist a perfect harmony between all entities, the individual person, the business and the life thereof. This is a one way entry ticket to the business world.

This book is if and when you want to embark on an entrepreneurial journey, and do not know where to begin, where to begin, and this is all you need to formulate that one time plan of attack.

The separation between business as a legal entity and an individual as an entrepreneur often cause controversial debates, questionable moralities and many other things.

This is a compass that shows you exactly where you want to be.

PART 1

THE 10 CARDINALS OF ENTREPRENEURIAL LIFE

I

There is only one thing you can start from the top that will actually work, that's digging a whole, and by the time you are done, you will be inside it, with no way out except to go back where you were before you began.

If I told you I met whoever you conceive to be God last night, I have absolutely no doubt you would not believe me. you would probably think I lost it, and this is not because you think I'm a liar, your decision to not believe me stems from years of what you have been taught, either by people or experience, it's not even conscious anymore. This is how a human mind works. Now, tell me! How do I teach you what you think you know already? Who told you what you think you know about business/entrepreneurship is the truth? How do you know the last thing you read on the subject is the truth? How do you know what you are hearing from me now is the truth? Do not believe or disbelieve what I'm telling you, just listen and maybe you might be able to do what you think, independent of your experience and education, just doing your thoughts.

The first thing is to realize how your mind was re-wired from the way it was when you were born, so that you can wire it according to your will. Currently, your mind have boundaries that you yourself have imposed on it, the most obvious being the mentality of right and wrong. Who says what is right or wrong? That which those around us find as unacceptable is automatically wrong, and those acceptable become right. With a few years of this judgements you will realise what someone believe, that which you do not, will automatically render that person a bad person, and those agreeing with your believe systems the good people. Thinking about it can this really be the case? That you are the benchmark and everyone who does not copy you is something else less than what you think you are?

School is very important, that's precisely why you have no problem reading and comprehending what I have written, but one must acknowledge that school teach us how to think and be effective or/and efficient at tasks, but as you keep on learning, the final stages of schooling teach us how to work, of course at a job/work that's already in existence, so if you decided perhaps on being an accountant, you are learning how to be a good one for a business that's already in existence, meaning you learn to work for someone, basically this is what you have been taught from birth and it's not even your thought, it's something that was thought of by someone, you are learning and perfecting how to use his/her thoughts, now, can you mentally put all those learning's to side and just listen to my madness for a while? Perhaps with a bit of thought, you can make your own thoughts and way.

You have believed what you believe for so long it has become a fabric of your very being, it's what defines you. Take a kid who grew up around entrepreneurs that struggled and perhaps were homeless at some stage for example, the kid will grow up thinking and believing you first have to suffer immensely to have money. This is why we say you are your environment. A mind learns what is, and come up with solutions or its own theories inspired by what was. Why do you think some people choose to become doctors or nurse after their parents or loved ones die at a hospital? How come most police officers come from crime ridden areas? We say your mind because it belongs to you. You are supposed to be in control of your mind, not it controlling you. You have already trained it to be in charge for ages with tons of your unfounded subconscious. Being ready to learn is going to be a mental battle which you have to conquer, it is only then that you can hear me. Do not judge, believe or disbelieve, just listen and perhaps find what is of value. This is why the Zen proverb attributed to both Gautama, the one you know as Buddha, and Lao Tzu, the great general say "when the student is ready, the teacher appears. When the student is truly ready, the teacher disappears" the teacher is here already, but are you ready to become a student? If not, then you would see another foolish student of life and not a teacher.

Have you realized yet how most motivational speakers/entrepreneurs always present what they call their truths? Some say they ate from bins, some were abused, and most didn't have any support. They had to start from rock bottom or they were drug addicts. How come we don't hear stories of how an ordinary person with ordinary life and ordinary problems rose to fame? Does it mean if you are above poverty line and happy with your life you are doomed as an entrepreneur? This can't possibly be the truth. The idea of a struggle was first born in their minds through experiences and observation; believe it or not it is them who manifested it to reality, they couldn't control their minds, they couldn't think themselves out of those situations then, it only happened at a later stage, and this is why it's a tale now.

There are tons of entrepreneurs, how then can there be only one manual on the subject with so many different people doing different things at different areas and times?

When you are ready to learn, no judging, believing or not believing, then hearing me out and understanding where I come from, this old fool might be able to teach you a thing or two, which perhaps might activate your way of thinking and a way of life.

Entrepreneurship today is not what is used to be. It's about what it can be. It's a way of life. It's a place where diversity, creativity, ideology, cutting edge, and future meets to address a need or want of some kind in return for something, be in monitory, satisfaction or otherwise that somehow enrich the entrepreneur (note there are variety of reasons people do business, some do it to continue the lineage or family values, some for the thrill of achieving the impossible, breaking boundaries, or merely to empower and help others, it's not always about the money). Though the methodologies and reasons for being in business have changed and evolved overtime, the principles remain the same.

Business has evolved significantly in the past and it constantly is. Change is the only thing that has been, is, and will always be constant and consistent in Business. Being armed with the relevant, effective and efficient mental tools is a must to make it in the current business world. Long gone are the days where tough, scary, old man's in black suits defined the business world.

Business has become less formal drastically over time, from presentation to communication. Now dressing to express you is a way to go, suits are no longer a daily business dress code. People seldom meet or email for minor things, they text, chat, tweet, etc. Even the way we communicate to get the point across, slang is often used to effectively allow common understanding and strengthen the business relationship. Business has changed with the times, we do not make profits anymore, we "secure the bag" and this is not how we do, this is how we "roll".

The new generation has took the business to the new level which is more convenient and effective for them. They do not trade during business hours anymore, their gadgets allow them to be in business one way or another at any time of the day in any place they wish. No one or place is beyond their reach, the world has become one small village, accessible with just a single click or a touch of a button, hence the term: business never sleeps. So relinquish all the thoughts of what you thought business was or is.

Technology has placed itself at a business center stage; employees and employers are dependent on their gadgets to make sound business decisions. It has become almost impossible to do business the traditional way. Travelling is not a necessity anymore; you can have a meeting from your bedroom with a person overseas. You do not even have to go to the bank to make a payment or to save nowadays, this is the digital era, accept it and bring yourself up to speed, this is the current reality.

Trying is the worst thing you can engage you mind on, either do or don't. It's entirely up to you, it is your life. No one owes you a push, support or anything of the sort. If you do get something along those lines, yes it's a bonus but also unnecessary pressure and focus derailment. Now you don't just worry about what you are doing, you also worry about someone else or some people, the disappointment if it doesn't go as planned and the wanting to make them proud, forget all that, do this for you and only you.

In the little history I was told, only one man was pushed and actually did something great, I hear his name was Jesus, as the story goes, apparently he was invited with his mother to some event when the host ran out of a drink. Jesus himself made peace with the fact that they ran out and accepted the fact as it, but his mother was having none of that, the man even said he wasn't ready and it wasn't yet time when his mother asked him to do something about it. The mother ignored all his ramblings and ordered the helpers to bring forth drums of water, told his son he knows what to do and left. Believe it or not the guy actually turned that water to wine, a good wine from what I heard. Can you believe it? The guy made wine out of just ordinary tap water! Okay maybe it was a fountain water and not tap water, but he still made wine out of water. If the mother had let him have it his way, people would have went home thinking ah the host tried but it wasn't enough, Then there wouldn't have been no such story, this man wouldn't have a reputation of making the finest wine out of pure water, there wouldn't even have been a record that such great man ever existed.

Although you may have/had a mother, be your own mother, push yourself. The time is never perfect; the next best thing is now. You are never going to be more ready than you are now. It's all in your mind. No time will ever be perfect and that's simply because the world is constantly in motion, you are never going to catch up to it. Trying is a foolish and futile exercise. You cannot know everything there is to know in just one lifetime, this is a way of life, and we learn as we live, same as the cow graze as its relieving itself. One of the great economists, Dr Peter Bouwer, once told me "in the long run, we are all dead", and he simply meant the now is the only thing we are sure of, even in a minute to come, all this will be history, we are alive and well now, and that's why we should do or not do, now! Be the case as it may, there will never be a golden moment like the now.

"Do or do not. There is no try", Yoda. With this being said: You know the saying "behind every successful man there is a woman and vies-a-versa?" well, this saying is true but not complete in business, it's more like 'behind every successful Entrepreneur there is family, friends, partner, society in which the business operates and everyone in his/her life'. Entrepreneurs are people, and people feel, they get hurt, sad and demotivated. Entrepreneurship is a highly psychological game, the 'I can do it attitude on its own won't cut it, you need psychological and emotional support (here is where the madness is starting to show with contradiction to some), and encouragement of those around you. You need someone/people to believe in you. You cannot make it if there is the element of negativity in your life, Imagine you are a stock trader and just as you open your computer, your partner tells you it will end in tears and everyone who is successful in that discipline is both a crock and a cheat. Negativity lasts longer than positivity, you cannot, amongst other things, afford to doubt yourself as an entrepreneur, give yourself reason to stay confident in your work as an entrepreneur, but be open to constructive criticism, surround yourself with ambitious and positive people all the time and stay motivated (you see? Now we are selective of people)

II

Firstly accept that you do not know anything about anything, what you know about anything is immaterial at most. If a man go study human behavior for years at school, can you honestly say that man is an expert on people? No he's not! He's just an expert on the subject. He doesn't know anything about people, and he won't until he lives amongst the people and experience all that he has learnt. He must perceive the behavior and what constituted such, hence we say you do not know anything about anything, all that you think you know is what you heard or read, you don't really know. Perception and experience is everything. This is why one can be genius and yet be absolutely clueless; the man simply doesn't know what he is talking about.

Borrowing a page from the mystics, we hear of a man called Vivekananda, who had a lengthy discussion and argument with one of the highly acclaimed philosopher of those times, so the discussion led them to the philosopher's office where he spoke very highly of the book that was on his table. Apparently the book had over 700 pages, so Vivekananda wanted to know more about this book since the man spoke so highly of it, he sold it so well it was almost as great as the Mahabharata. Vivekananda was hungry to know more about it, so he asked the man to give him an hour with the book, the man burst in to laughter wondering how possible can Vivekananda know anything about the book within an hour especially considering the book was in German and Vivekananda did not speak German. After some time he indulged him and gave the book, Vivekananda simply held the book in his palms and closed his eyes, in an hour he gave the book and his comment was the book does not contain anything of value. The man thought how arrogant is this guy, the book is in German, he didn't speak German, he did not even look at the book or at least open it, Vivekananda sensing the man's disgust he told the man to ask him anything on any page and he will say it as is, so the man tried a few pages and Vivekananda repeated it to the man as it was, he was so intrigues he had to ask how he hid it, what sorcery was this? Vivekananda said: "this is why they call me Vivekananda". Perception! By merely touching the book, Vivekananda being the yogi that he was, he perceived everything that was on the book. Nothing has to make sense to you, nothing you read can be confirmed as the ultimate truth or lie, you have to perceive it and experience it yourself, and then you can truly say you know. An African proverb clearly states 'An adult squatting, see further than a child on a tree'. Perception and experience. You can never know too much or more than everyone. Yes you have acquired the knowledge at school or over the years, but you will not know until you have been through that.

III

Presentation is everything in business, from the way you dress to the way you pitch your business. Though business has become less formal over the past years, good-looking is still something that weighs a lot, you can't just wakeup in the morning and go to a Business meeting without bathing or in your overalls. Fashion is a way of making a statement without speaking a word, but by the way you have dressed, we can tell a lot about you. Imagine if you want a person who loves animals to invest in your business and you go to a meeting dressed in clothing made from animal skin, especially animals that are about to be extinct, you have failed before you even lift a finger, more likely than not, that meeting won't even start.

Another important thing is how you behave before, during and after the presentation, you can't keep scratching you head or keep shifting on your seat during the presentation; work on your nerves, be calm and at peace, being nervous make you look like you do not know what you are talking about.

What we mean by before and after presentation is your way of life, you have got to live your business, be the ambassador of you brand. How do you think the meeting is going to go if you get there and you realize the guy you are meeting is the same guy you shouted "what the hell are you doing? I'm not riding your mother's cow, what? Did your mother give you your driving license? Huh? The cat got your tongue?" at the robot on your way to the meeting? Behave like a professional always. If you have issues, deal with them the best way you know how professionally, if you can't, then it's easy, seek help. As a golden rule, if you wouldn't want people knowing about it, then don't do it at all.

Business presentation is the subject at hand, this is what you have come for, and it is no less for the person you are making a presentation to. Preparation is the key here, no matter how much you know about your business. You must prepare and rehearse you presentation several times before the actual presentation. You only have one meeting to convince whoever you want to convince, this is your only chance, the person is willing to listen, see, change and make mind, hence they agreed to meet with you for the presentation, do not disappoint, once you disappoint, they will remember that forever, and even if you have something better next time, they will regard it as a total waste of time, and yes! Time is money. That person/people have sacrificed some important things to come hear what you have got to say. And always remember, "You will never get a second chance to make a first impression".

IV

Dead hay carries the seed of new hay, same is true for people. If we follow Charles Darwin's theory that we evolved from some sort of Ape or Monkeys, whatever his case was, clearly this means we as people got better and better over time, even our intellects, now I know some may ask how come then do we still have monkeys and why haven't they too transformed, were they less smarter or what procedure was followed, this isn't the point, the point is we got smarter and smarter over time. We are at a level where most of the animals' instincts and behaviour have been suppressed to almost none existence.

From our very beginning to now, we can see why and how we have become smarter than any other animal in the planet, but be the case as it may, there can never be an end of evolution, meaning we should always strive to evolve more. I personally believe it is an insult to both whoever you call your God or Ancestors to not strive for more. Generation after generation of your ancestors have worked very hard to become better, and you are their final product, it will be a waste of millions of years of progress if you were to become anything less than what they were.

It is your birth right to do better and become better, for you know better. Your ancestors lived at the times of caves, exes and rivers, you live at the time of sky scrapers, don't set the entire generational progress back by your lack of ambition, build your castle, tallest sky scrapper or whatever you desire, nature sacrificed all of them so you can be here, so act like it, do better, keep evolving.

V

People often hide their lack of action and ambition behind lack of knowledge or inexperience. If you have no experience then great, you have nothing to hold you back, for the very first time you have an advantage over everyone else. Do you have any idea how hard it is to work against what you know to be the truth? Both knowledge and experience?

Knowledge is an unnecessary burden, imagine if I said you were walking all wrong and what you must do is move your legs sideways, do you have any ideas how hard you will struggle? But that will be a piece of cake for a kid without any knowledge or experience of walking, both experience and knowledge is a hindrance, In any task you perform, both knowledge and experience will kick in making it extremely difficult to think of anything different from the norm. Being inexperienced means your thinking is already broadened, nothing to get in a way of you applying yourself to thee best of your abilities, that's very hard for someone with experience.

Besides, have you really thought what experience is? You learn something, then repeat that thing over a prolonged period of time, basically you are getting 1 day of experience since you only have to learn that for a day, repeat that for 10 more years and you have 10 years' worth of experience, isn't that a wasted time and opportunity? Unlearn all you have learnt. school is one way of mentally handicapping yourself, you will only think of what is from your knowledge on the subject, on what you have been taught, isn't that a waste considering the evolutionary process that took place so you can learn to think for yourself? The purpose of education or books should only be seen as a way of realising what other people (the author) think regarding the matter at hand, not to replace or suppress your own ability to think for yourself.

VI

Can you comprehend the logic that sorghum beer stored in a wine bottle doesn't make it wine? When I was taught traditional healing, there was a point I healed a few people who most thought couldn't be healed and their time was up, so my teacher realised that will hinder my learning and only achieve the one thing he have been avoiding all this time, me having a big head and thinking I'm some sort of a God.

So he called me to his little hut like he usually did when he had stories to tell or some lesson, he asked what I thought of my gift(ability to heal), I told him I fell its growing and soon I will be the most powerful healer around, he asked what happened to the first lesson he gave, the lesson on being humble whatever praise or disappointments one got from helping people, so he said, "look: forget all the lessons for now, I am your teacher, I had a teacher, if you are as powerful as you think you are, then how powerful are we since we are the ones imparting this lessons to you"? "mighty" I said. "I understand", he said: "my son, here is a lesson for tonight, remember it to your last breath, so even when I am with my ancestors, I will be watching to make sure you learnt this, this is the most important and most powerful lesson out of everything we have talked about, this is how you raise the dead, this is how you become the Man-God, are you ready"? 'yes sir' I said with joy, "My son, if you ever feel powerful, even if it's just a thought, and you realise you are the greatest, then you should in that instant, go to the mountain and make the stream flow up the river, just one stream, even if it's the tiniest. You may not understand me now, but someday you will."

VII

The use of language plays an important role in making or breaking an Entrepreneur, it is not about being right or wrong; it's about doing what is regarded as "morally correct and acceptable". For example, most societies in South Africa are able to live with the ideology of Abortion simply because it is legal and they do not want to be called discriminatory/racists/the offender of women's rights. Though they may not say it aloud, this is a very sensitive and morally unacceptable issue to date, you may not even utter a word about it in some societies, so most people see it as wrong though they may not prosecute you for it, it is considered morally wrong.

With its diverse cultures and believe systems, it is often hard to know what is morally right or wrong in South Africa, a simple look in the eye while greeting may mean you are rude, arrogant and too proud in some societies, while not looking in some may mean you are a witch, you lack guards or you are mourning a loved one. One must be sensitive especially to cultural and religious issues of the society one interact/do business with and/or around.

VIII

Racing on the streets, the challenge is not really winning; the challenge is staying alive while doing it. For example, if safety isn't an issue and you really want to win, then you simply have to cut your brakes and ride. The above can be understood as: whilst striving for the top, do not take short cuts, take the long road there, even if the red tape can be avoided with calling on a few people and making a few donations or whatever you may call it, do not do it, it will set you back to less than where you started. This game is more about you than your product/service itself, so your reputation is and should be your most valuable asset, how people perceive you as an individual. Most even accumulate a reputation through association, so scrutinize who you are dealing with. E.g. How do you expect us to be in business with you or trust us with our money while you socialize with pyramid scheme founders, corrupt politician and/or drug dealers? What will we think of you? It is a general assumption that birds of the same feathers flock together. Guard your reputation, your reputation is your life. I have closed deals that looked impossible to close even to me by just reputation. Mentally programmed with the "do not bite the hand that feeds you", we often find it hard to say "no" to the person who provides our financial security, the one who has the power to make or break our careers and/or financial stability, more so in this ever tough economic climate where employment/Entrepreneurship is associated with luck. The abuse of one's power either by delegation or being autocratic is both illegal and unethical, the worst of this being using your position or power to make and get sexual advances from the employees/colleagues.

IX

Ethicality has remained an issue in business over the years, and this is exactly why and how most people taint their reputations. The way an entrepreneur conduct him/herself in and out of the work environment is of utmost importance, entrepreneurs must learn to live their profession. We all are human but one must learn to live according to the general code of Ethics and be in good conduct at all times. The most important as mentioned is sexual conduct of an entrepreneur in and out of the business. It seems most entrepreneur have in the past practiced improper behavior especially in the work place. Entrepreneurs have exchanged work related incentives and opportunities for sex, this is not just unethical; it is a disgrace to the business profession. Sexual harassment have remained an issue over the years, being sexually harassed can be verbal, physical and emotional, one can be harassed by getting emails with sexual content, or those that suggest such, it can be by being touched, etc. play far from such and those accused of such.

X

I have often argued that discipline should be taught as a subject at school to at least inspire a different kind of thinkers. We have seen those whom we have thought intelligent, those we have held in high regard due to their success, those we call educated, they all fail due to one thing, discipline! If we truly are those who have evolved from animal kingdom, then where does this kind of thinking and disruptive behaviour come from? I certainly have never seen an animal that was so proficient that it killed so many animals it had to howl and call other animals to all come feast with it.

We have not just heard, but we have seen the stories that should have been stories of inspiration and hope become classical example of how one can be educated or considered wise in some discipline and still be stupid beyond measure.

It has been said that more than half of the highly paid sports and entertainment personalities who amongst all odds fought to become the best ever and highly paid in their respective discipline have went back to being poor just a few years after their retirement, 5 years to be exact. The lottery winners? Apparently even a year is too much as a millionaire, 8 months at most is enough for many to go back to poverty. Of all currently employed, research shows that only a tenth of them can retire financially independent.

We grew up watching people struggle to be regarded as someone in communities. We have seen the struggle people have endured to try and make their lives better off, yet the story always have the same ending. We see doctors, directors, lawyers, even pastors who worked so hard to get where they are become just another statistic with a bit of money, they get a few thousands then suddenly they throw away their responsibilities, dreams and ways of life, they buy cars, party day and night, accumulate more debt since such access is now on their fingertips, and flex on the very same community one should be uplifting, there is no investments whatsoever, only hand to mouth, get paid and spend, that's it!

Before you know it, one is suffering from major depression, cannot execute any work as before due to stress, they lose weight, suddenly becomes bitter and almost always start saying things like when days are dark friends are few. They start blaming people in their very circle for deserting them, etc. but the root of all this is lack of financial discipline and simple financial literacy.

Financial freedom is a choice, dare I say it, even if you make a choice of not choosing, you still made a choice of not choosing. Money requires discipline, and like any other thing, it needs a proper plan. One should discipline one's self to avoid unnecessary spending and rather focus the spending on things that bring in more money. Failure to have a proper plan as history dictates leads to suicide, depression, indignity and inevitably early death.

The signs are always and will always be present, eg.spending way more than you earn, which will lead to loans which will often be unbearable to pay.

On the issue of spending, if you do not have a budge to follow, you have already failed and fell in to the trap. Create a budget and follow it to the death. A budget is a plan of spending, without which it's like going to a place you have never been without a map. A budget must cover all the cost you make constantly and/or periodically together the money received and expected. By having a budget, you will know exactly how you spent and on what. The plans you make for the future and currently should always be provided for in a budget, below is an example of how and where to begin.

MONTHLY BUDGET

JUNE 2010

		PLANNED
INCOME(before tax)		22700
Fixed income	17500	
Salary	15000	
Rent income	2500	
Variable income	2700	
Chicken sales	900	
Trailer hire	1800	
Share dividend	2500	
Tax deductible income		-2500
Share dividends	-2500	
Taxable income		20200
tax	-3000	-3000
Non-taxable income	-2500	-2500
TOTAL NETT INCOME		19700
Investments		-6000
Chicken coup	1500	
Share portfolio	2000	
Rental houses	2500	
Smart spend		-3000
Medical aid	500	
Life insurance	550	
Car insurance	1200	
House insurance	750	
Expenses		
Fixed		-2150
Dstv	350	
Phone contract	1000	
Rates and taxes	800	
Variable		-9000
Water & electricity	1000	
Car service	3000	
Petrol	1500	
Cow feeds	1500	
grocery	1500	
entertainment	500	-20150
TOTAL EXPERNDITURE		
DISPOSABLE INCOME		-450

This is an example of a budget. A planned monthly expenditure, you should have a yearly plan, half year, quarterly and monthly plans. The above shows clearly what the writer plan to spend during the month of June. He/she recorded all the income expected and expense expected, notice that one must always have notes to the budget, eg, under expenses is a grocery with expected purchase value of 1500, this is what is planned to spend on grocery. But how does one come up with such a figure? Everything must be planned to the t; notes on grocery can be the following as an example:

2kgRice

5kgCarrots

100Tea bags

5kgSugar

1Bag of potatoes

5kg of chicken

2kg pork ribs

500g salt, etc

Taking 1500 and going shopping without such a list leads to irresponsibility, you know what you consume and how much can last you a full month. Going without a list will waste your time and you will end up purchasing unnecessary things, things you might have at home already. This is to show you a budget should be something you visit constantly, eg, when you see you are about to run out of salt, put it on the list already, and before going out shopping, check if everything else is still available, there is no use going to the shops with an incomplete list, that's more waste than initially intended because you will need another time, petrol and money to go make another shopping during the month. Prepare your budget based on realistic values, you have internet if you are not sure how much what will cost.

Budget is not just a written paper; it's a way of life that must be followed with a passion and discipline. So assuming the budget is done, how does one know if everything is as planned? Although one might plan his/her spending, that is all we can be responsible for, we don't set prices on goods, therefore there are bound to be variations or difference between planned spending and what is actually spent, for example, one cannot estimate the price of fuel with certainty for it can increase or decrease during the month thereby disrupting one's plan.

However, be that as it may, the variations and reasons thereof after spending should be addressed by clearly indicating why the spending went overboard or was drastically reduced compared to what was forecasted on the plan. You must do that for your own good, you must hold yourself accountable and correct any unnecessary variations by understanding reasons for such, with a budget not being followed disregarded as a reason, that's not a reason, its disrespect to yourself and an insult to those who believe in you, its immaturity and irresponsibility to discipline yourself to follow your own words, its self-sabotage. Budget is a life plan, a financial life plan, and therefore should be treated as such. A budget after spending, noticing and reporting variations to yourself or your partner will more or overlook as follows:

		PLANNED	ACTUAL	DIVIATION	REASON
INCOME(before tax)		22700	22700	0	
Fixed income	17500				
Salary	15000				
Rent income	2500				
Variable income	2700				
Chicken sales	900				
Trailer hire	1800				
Share dividend	2500				
Tax deductible income		-2500	-2500	0	
Share dividends	-2500				
Taxable income		20200	20200	0	
tax	-3000	-3000	-3000	0	
Non-taxable income		2500	2500		
TOTAL NETT INCOME		19700	19700	0	
Investments		-6000	-6000	0	
Chicken coup	1500				
Share portfolio	2000				
Rental houses	2500				
Smart spend		-3000	-3000	0	
Medical aid	500				
Life insurance	550				
Car insurance	1200				
House insurance	750				
Expenses					
Fixed		-2150	-2150	0	
Dstv	350				
Phone contract	1000				
Rates and taxes	800				
Variable		-9000	7800	1200	
Water & electricity	1000		750	250	Less usage
Car service	3000		2750	250	Billed less
Petrol	1500		2100	-600	Trip home
Cow feeds	1500		900	600	Sale
grocery	1500		1200	300	Most available
entertainment	500		100	400	Did not go out
TOTAL EXPERNDITURE		-20150	18950	1200	Due to above
DISPOSABLE INCOME		-450	750		

Any individual should have a point of reference, something to back up your progress and something to show us who you are financially, in case you need to borrow money for whatever reason you may, this is what is called a credit report. A credit report shows us amongst other things if you are a good payer or a bad payer, it also show us how much debt you have and your whole borrowing history, if you qualify for credit or not.

Not having any debts is bad as we cannot establish with certainty if you can afford to pay us back since you have no history of paying or borrowing from anyone, this does not mean having loads of debt is good either, this can make it impossible for you to make any more borrowing or even make a simple living.

Below is an example of a credit report:

CONSUMER CREDIT REPORT

Enquiry Input Details

Enquiry Date	01/01/2020 - 00:10:20
Enquiry Type	Consumer Credit Enquiry
Subscriber Name	Moletsane and Partners (pty) Ltd
Subscriber User Name	Moletsane K.E
Enquiry Input	0101010000083	Vergetta
Enquiry Reason	Credit assessment

PERSONAL DETAILS SUMMARY

This section displays the Personal information for the consumer. Included here are: ID or Passport, Name, Gender, Marital Status, Current Contact, Address, and Employment Info

Reference No.	ABC78782	External Reference No.	
ID No.	0101010000083	Passport or 2nd ID No.	
Surname	VERGETTA	Residential Address	
First Name	ELLIAS	Postal Address	PRIVATE BAG X10111, ZEERUST, 2880
Second Name	STANDER	Telephone No. (H)	
Title	Professor	Telephone No. (W)	
Gender	Male	Cellular/Mobile	
Date of Birth	2001-01-01	E-mail Address	
Marital Status	Single	Current Employer	Mosupatsela Investments(pty)ltd

POTENTIAL FRAUD INDICATORS

This section displays information verified by Home Affairs.

ID No. Verified Status At Home Affairs	Yes
ID No. Deceased Status At Home Affairs	No
ID No. Found on Fraud Database	No access- SAFPS Members only

BSS PRESAGE

The BSS Presage score is a generic bureau scorecard which indicates the credit risk associated with a consumer by taking into consideration the consumer's historical credit profile and repayment behavior. The higher the score, the lower the associated risk of future payment delinquency or default.

DEBT SUMMARY

This section displays a summary of all the consumer's current debt obligations, legal enforcement action taken, Court Notices, enquiries done on this consumer by credit providers and debt counseling information.

Description	NLR	CPA
Total number of accounts active	1	0
Total No. of Accounts in Good Standing	1	0
Total No. of Accounts In Arrears	0	0
Total number of accounts paid-up	S	0
Total Monthly Instalments	R 3099	R 0
Total Outstanding Debt	R 35 266	R 0
Total Arrear Amount	R 0	R 0
Highest Months in Arrears (Last 24 Months)	5	0
Total Adverse Amount (Write offs/Repossessions)	R 0	R 0
Total Enquiries Done in the last 90 days by Subscriber	R 0	0

Description	Total	Amount
Public Domain - Adverse / Defaults	0	R 0
BSS Default listing	0	R 0
Judgments	0	R 0
Court Notices (Admin Orders/Sequestrations/Rehabilitation Orders)	0	R 0
Enquiries (last 24 months)	0	
Current Property Interests	0	R 0
Total No of Principal Links (CIPC)	0	
Debt Review Status		
Dispute Information		
Total Enquiries Done in the last 90 days by Other Subscribers	0	0
Total No. of Accounts opened within the last 45 days	0	0

PAYMENT PROFILE: CREDIT ACCOUNT STATUS

This section includes 24 month payment behavior of all credit agreements as reported by the Credit Grantors belonging to Credit Providers Association (CPA).

PAYMENT PROFILE: NATIONAL LOANS REGISTER-NLR

This section includes 24 month payment behavior of all credit agreements as reported by Micro Lenders as part of the National Loans Register (NLR).

Date Account Opened	Company	Account No.	Loan Amount	Current Balance	Instalment Amount	Arrears Amount	Type of Account	Current Status of Account	Last Paid Date
18-01-27	X	36B3F	R 2 366	R 0	R 0	R 0	K	Closed	19-06-26
18-11-25	X	6495	R 481	R 0	R 0	R 0	K	Closed	18-12-23
18-09-27	X	6273G	R 3	R 0	R 0	R 0	K	Closed	18-10-21
18-09-27	X	6B92R	R 46 280	R 35 366	R 3060	R 0	K	Active	19-12-25
17-03-06	X	5467D	R 44 108	R 0	R 0	R 0	K	Closed	18-06-06
16-12-08	X	5613R	R 30 000	R 0	R 0	R 0	K	Closed	17-03-06

- 1   Unsecured Payday loan

- 2,3,4   Unsecured Term loan

- K   Unsecured Term Loan

- P   Personal Cash Loan

- J   Unsecured Revolving Loan

MONTHLY PAYMENT BEHAVIOUR AS AT 01-01-2020

Company	J	D	N	O	S	A	J	J	M	A	M	F	J	D	N	O	S	A	J	J	M	A	M	P
X	#	#	#	#	#	#	#	C	3	2	1	1	0	#	#	#	#	#	#	#	#	#	#	0
X	#	#	#	#	#	#	#	#	#	#	#	#	C	0	#	#	#	#	#	#	#	#	#	#
X	#	#	#	#	#	#	#	#	#	#	#	#	#	#	C	0	#	#	#	#	#	#	#	#
X	#	0	0	0	0	0	#	5	4	3	2	1	0	0	0	0	0	#	#	#	#	#	#	#
X	#	#	#	#	#	#	#	#	#	#	#	#	#	#	#	C	0	0	0	0	0	0	#
X	#	#	#	#	#	#	#	#	#	#	#	#	#	#	#	#	#	#	#	#	#	C	0

Definitions	Indicators
No data found	#
Repeat of previous month's Status Code	*
Not in arrears	0
No of months in arrears	1-9
Closed	C
Terms Extended	E
Paid Up	P

PUBLIC DOMAIN RECORDS

This section displays all details of Court Notices, Judgments, Legal enforcement action taken by credit providers and debt review status.

ADVERSE/DEFAULTS

* Nothing on Record

BSS DEFAULT LISTING

* Nothing on Record

JUDGEMENTS

* Nothing on Record

COURT NOTICE

* Nothing on Record

ADMINISTRATION ORDERS

* Nothing on Record

SEQUESTRATION AND PROVISIONAL SEQUESTRATIONS

* Nothing on Record

REHABILITATION ORDERS

* Nothing on Record

DEBT REVIEW STATUS

* Nothing on Record

BSS PAYMENT NOTIFICATIONS

This section displays default payment alerts loaded for early and late stage collections for non-performing accounts

CONSUMER INFORMATION

This section supplies a list of current and previous addresses, contact and employment data.

ADDRESS HISTORY

Bureau Update	Type	Line 1	Line 2	Postal code
2019-01-01	Postal	PRIVATE BAG X10111, ZEERUST, 2880	ZEERUST	2880
2019-01-01	Postal	P.O.Box 530	ZEERUST	2870

CONTACT HISTORY
    * Nothing on Record

Email ADDRESS
    * Nothing on Record

EMPLOYMENT HISTORY

Bureau Update	Employer	Designation
2017-08-16	Mosupatsela Investments(pty)ltd	Financial Master

CREDIT ENQUIRY HISTORY
This section includes a list of organizations or credit providers who have requested a Credit Report on this consumer.

PROPERTY INTERESTS
This section displays a list of properties registered in the name of the consumer at the Deeds offices around SA.

PRINCIPAL LINKS
This section displays a list of companies where the consumer is linked as a principal.

The above credit report is self-explanatory, we can see clearly how much this man have and how much he has taken before, where he currently is in terms of payments and how many debts he have settled before, this credit report is fairly ok, however, to be able to judge him fairly, we have to establish his affordability as we can see on the behavior section that he has skipped a few payments before. Affordability takes in to account all your income, deduct all your monthly expenses and investments and current loan payments, whatever is left after that, is the amount you can afford to pay regardless of how much you are borrowing.

Assuming a monthly income of about R10000, with expenses and loan payments of R8200, then my affordability will be the balance, which is R1800. This is why people may need to borrow say R100000 and the bank or lending institution is offering way less, affordability is everything as we(the lenders) have to establish you can pay us without any trouble.

I do not plan on you making a mess of your financials, therefore I will not discuss what to do when you run into financial troubles, more so debts, however, there are many options should such occur, but as evident as it is on the above credit report, it will be a temporary prison. Eg, one of such solutions is debt counseling.
With such, your payments will be reduced drastically based on your affordability, however, this means for a period you are under debt counseling you cannot accumulate more debt, act as a company director as per the current rules, and cannot make any major purchases that would otherwise require large funding like a mortgage.

For now, should you need a breather, scale down on your expenses and use more cost saving methods and inherit cost saving habits, eg, reduce going out, reduce alcohol consumption, shop at discounted stores and stay out of your expensive habits.

PART 2

READING FINANCIAL STATEMENTS

WHAT ARE THE FINANCIAL STATAMENTS?

Financial Statements are Summarized Financial Reports on Business Performance and operations over a specified period (normally a year) of time.

These reports however, to allow common understanding between users, are prepared according to IFRS (International Financial Reporting Standards) prescribed standards and format tailored to cater for wide range of users interested in reading these financial statements.

WHO ARE THEY PREPARED FOR?

Financial statements are prepared for every one with any kind of interest in the Business (Stakeholders). People base their financial opinions about the business on these reports.

The following are, but not limited to, stakeholders in any business;

Shareholders (Owners/Investors)

Employees (Workers)

Loaners/Lenders

Suppliers and people owed by Business

Customers and Clients

General Public

The Government and its Agencies

WHY ARE THEY IMPORTANT? (Financial Statements)

Without the Financial statements, obtaining financial information about most businesses will be nearly impossible. Financial statements therefore provide information about financial performance and changes in these performances over time, It is through this reports that we know if the business made any income or not and for how long. Almost all entrepreneurs, Investors and Financing Institutions make their decisions about the business after evaluating these reports; some even go as far as predicting the future with these reports

UNDERSTSNDING TERMS AND WORDING USED IN THE FINANCIAL STATEMENTS

Assets -Belongings of a business in general (Property of any kind)

Official definition-Resources controlled by the entity as results of past events and from which future economic benefits are expected to flow to the entity.

Resource-is a something whether tangible/not that is worth some economic value.
Control-refer to the right to be able to use the assets as the business please and all the benefits of the asset in question belong to the business for the duration of such asset.
Past events-refer to the procedure or way used to acquire the asset in question (commonly purchase)
Future economic benefits-The benefits of using such assets that can be measured in form of money
Flow to the entity-the entity gain something worth some economic value

Current Assets -Property that can be disposed or used in less than a year or so

Non Current Assets   -Property of longer life time than a year including those permanent

Liabilities   -Debts/Money owed by the business to any party

Official definition-present obligations of the entity arising from past events, the settlements of which is expected to result in an outflow from the entity of resources embodying economic benefits.

Present obligation-the entity is legally obliged to honor the debt (it owes someone/ some business something)
Past events-refer to the time of acquiring/making the obligation
Settlement-that is the payment/honoring of the debt or whatever performance worth economic value disclosed
Outflow from entity (economic benefits)-the settlement there of will result in a decrease in the bank balance or any other specified asset

Current Liabilities-Debts/Money owed by business but expected to be paid before the end of the current year of business

Non-Current Liabilities-Loans/ Money owed by business, which is expected to be paid in a period longer than a year
Receivables-Money expected to be received in less than a year
Payables-Money expected to be paid in far less than a year

Income

Official definition-are the increase in economic benefits during the accounting period in the form of inflows/enhancements of assets or decrease of liabilities that result in increase in equity, other than those relating to contribution from equity participants

Expenses

Official definition-Are decrease in economic benefits during the accounting period in the form of outflow or depletion of Assets or incurrence of liabilities that results in decrease in equity, other than those relating to distribution to equity participants.

Equities -Total Ownership of Business

Official definition-it is the residual interest in the Assets of the entity after deducting all its Liabilities
Share Capital & Reserves-Summarized share ownership and its worth

Balance Sheet-Summary of Financial Operations and stability of the Business (Shown with comparative figures), it's over a long term.

Income Statement-Shows performance of the Business over a short stipulated period
Revenue-This are money made on all sales mad (paid for and owed)

Cost of Sales-Costs incurred on goods sold (paid for and owed)

Gross Profit-Income received on total sales made

Profit before Tax-Total Income received/expected before paying Tax

Profit after Tax-Income left after paying Tax and everything else

Subsidiary-Business that is owned by another

Cash Flow Statement-Statement/Report on cash operations/flow of money in the Business (received and paid) for a stated period

Statement of changes in Equity-It shows change in ownership of the business over a specified period of time

Official Format of financial statements

For every element that goes in to the financial statements, the preparer must be certain that it is probable that future economic will flow to/from the entity and the value of that specific element can be measured with certainty and reliability. More or over, we put an element in to the financial statement only, and only if it meet the definition of that specific element.

ENTITY NAME		
Description of financial statement and the date of report issue		

	Previous year currency	Current year currency
ASSETS		
Non-Current Assets		
Current Assets		
TOTAL ASSETS		
EQUITIES AND LIABILITIES		
Equity		
LIABILITIES		
Non-Current Liabilities		
Current Liabilities		
TOTAL EQUITIES AND LIABILITIES		

Example

MOLETSANE K E PROFFESIONAL SERVICES		
Statement of Financial position as at 31December 2011		

	2010 R	2011 R
ASSETS		
Non-Current Assets	100 000	200 000
Current Assets	50 000	75 000
TOTAL ASSETS	150 000	275 000
EQUITIES AND LIABILITIES		
Equity	50 000	175 000
LIABILITIES		
Non-Current Liabilities	35 000	30 000
Current Liabilities	65 000	70 000
TOTAL EQUITIES AND LIABILITIES	150 000	275 000

Assets and liabilities are used to measure the position of the Entity Financially.

ENTITY NAME		
Description of financial statement and the date of report issue		

	Year	Year
	Currency	Currency
Revenue		
Cost of Sale		
Gross Profit		
Operating costs		
Gross Profit(before tax)		
Tax Expense		
Profit for the period		

Example

MOLETSANE K E PROFFESIONAL SERVICES		
Statement of Financial performance for the year ended 31December 2011		

	2010	2011
	R	R
Revenue	20 000	19 000
Cost of Sale	(10 000)	(9 500)
Gross Profit	10 000	9 500
Operating costs	(6 500)	(6 400)
Gross Profit(before tax)	3 500	3 100
Tax Expense	(11 750)	(1 030)
Profit for the period	2 325	2 070

Income and Expenses are most common elements used to measure profit and financial performance of the entity over a short period of time.

Gross Profit=Sales (Revenue)-Cost of sales. And from this:

Cost of Sales (stock/total production cost) = Sales (Revenue)- Gross Profit, and
Total Sales (Revenue) made= Cost of sales + Gross Profit

MAKING SENSE OF THE NUMBERS

To be able to determine if business has grown over time, and how much is this growth if it has even grew, or even determining its cycle, you need to be able to read and understand certain basic calculations. The following formulas are, amongst many, important in making sense of numbers in financial statements;

Percentage change-This is used to show movement overtime, be it growth or shrinking.
%change= {new (current)-old (previous)}/old (previous)
For example, if we were to calculate growth in Total Assets of Moletsane K E Professional Services now, it will be as follows (From Example.1)
%change= {new (current)-old (previous)}/old (previous)
= {275 000-150 000}/150000
=125 000/150 000
=0.83
0.83 is the same as 83%, we can therefore confidently say from 2010 to the end of 2011; Moletsane K E Professional Services have had an 83% growth in total Assets.
Using the same example we will calculate the growth in just Non Current Assets.
%change= {new (current)-old (previous)}/old (previous)
= {30 000-35000}/35 000
= {-5000}/35 000
=-0.14, same as -14%
Since the number is negative, we know negative growth is not possible, meaning this is not growth, and since negative is the opposite of positive, it means this is the opposite of growth; we have had a shrinking/ reduction in our total Noncurrent liabilities.

So whenever we use this formula and the answer is positive, it means it's a growth, and whenever is a negative, it means it has declined.

NOTES TO THE FINANCIAL STATEMENTS

This is exactly what the heading say, the notes; it is the explanation of how they got the numbers presented in the Statements presented. The following is an example of how Noncurrent assets were compiled for the financial year ended 31December 2011;

Noncurrent assets as at 31December 2010	R 150 000
Scrapped Vehicle as at 22June 2011	R (R90 000)
New Vehicle bought 13August 2011	R 160 000
Depreciation on Vehicles for the whole year	R (20 000)
Total Noncurrent assets as at 31December 2011	R200 000

SOCIAL RESPONSIBILITY AND CORPORATE GOVERNANCE REPORTING

Social responsibility means the business becomes an active member of the society it operates in, members of business community are:
Employees of that business
Government and its agencies
Lenders
Investors and financiers
General community that the business serve.

Business should report on the role they played on uplifting and empowering community, especially the previously disadvantaged groups, though this is not a legal requirement, it is a common practice.
Business must also be more cautious to the environment. As global warming is the burning issue now, it is worth reporting on, businesses must adopt technology and/or means that have less carbon emission. Everyone is going green.

THE BUSINESS
PROFILE AND PLAN

To succeed in business, be it a project, proposal, presentation or every day running of the business, you need a surefire strategy; and this, is a solid business plan.

In order to allow one to make an investment and/or financing decision, a Business plan must, among others, give its reader a clear picture of the business, product & product growth expected over time, customer base and behavior, rate of return, capital base, strategy, risks, the place of business in the market, its expected and current market share and customers, an overview of management and their expertise.

Lastly, an effective business plan must be clear on the following:
Its credit record.
Its ability to pay any future debts, especially the proposed loan.
The collateral, its value, details of the valuator and the state of that particular collateral.
Long term liabilities and equity composition.
Existing and expected market share.
Contingency plans and legal challenges.

The good thing about writing a Business Plan is the fact that there is no right or wrong way of doing it, there is no format, everything you deem necessary to achieve whatever motive you have to draft a business plan goes.

The rule is to keep it short and simple, maximum of 2 lines for a point, Stick to points only, no one have time to read through a pointless bible sized document.

Thorough research of business and its environment must be conducted with careful consideration and practice of highly recommended understandable statistical methods as this estimates are what makes a business plan. Most investors/entrepreneurs/financiers are financially literate, so numbers and graphs for their attraction is a must as they are probably the only thing that will make sense to them.

Be clear and factual when it comes to the numbers, they/we want to know about all the costs and returns expected in the business/project.

We recommend the following basic format:

Cover page
Table of contents
Executive summary and Entrepreneurial team
Description of business concept and the industry
Market analysis
Marketing plan
SWOT analysis
Finance plan and Budgets
Operation/Production plan
Competition
External environment risks
Legal Requirements and applicable regulations impact on business
Appendices and Business documents.
Here is an example:

BUSINESS PROFILE

OF

MOLETSANE STRATEGIC BUSINESS SOLUTIONS
ACCOUNTANTS, BOOKKEEPERS, CONSULTANTS (SMME), BUSI-
NESS MENTORS, AGENTS AND TAX PRACTITIONERS

INDEX

ENTITY NAME	: MOLETSANE STRATEGIC BUSINESS SOLUTIONS
TYPE OF SERVICE	: Professional Services
TYPE OF ENTITY	: Entrepreneurship
AREAS OF SPECIALITY	: SMME Consulting
	Accounting and Bookkeeping
	Tax Computing and Planning
	Project Management
	Presentation and Tutoring (SMME)
	Business Agents
	Business registration
	Name shelving
	BEE certificate registration
	Leadership, motivation and Business Seminars
FOUNDER/ACTIVE MEMBER	: Moletsane Kagiso Emmanuel
ENTITY REG NUMBER (SARS)	: 880816 1234 567
TAX PRACTITIONER NUMBER	: PC-C0B1234
TAX PAYER NUMBER	: 1043/208/15/4
CONTACT PERSON	: Moletsane Kagiso Emmanuel
CONTACT NUMBER (CELL)	: 072 123 4567
E-MAIL ADDRESS	: Laporzito@gmail.com
PHYSICAL ADDRESS	: 123b Borakalalo Village
	Lehurutshe
POSTAL ADDRESS	: P O BOX 530
	Motswedi
AREA & POSTAL CODE	: 2870

MOLETSANE STRATEGIC BUSINESS SOLUTIONS Is a Team of Highly Qualified Professionals Committed to Achieving High Standards of Competency and Professionalism.

We Specialize in;

SMME consulting
Business/Entrepreneurial coaching and mentoring,
Accounting and Bookkeeping,
Agency/Representation,
General Taxation issues,
Project Management,
Presentation and Tutoring (SMME),
Business registration and deregistration
Name shelving
BEE certificate registration

Be with us and have a piece of mind in your everyday business dealings.

We do contract work, meaning you do not have to bind yourself/business to long term obligations in case your financial stability/cycle changes, or merely want to change or restructure your operations.

To SMME's, new entrepreneurs, Commercial Students and any interested party in Business, We are a platform in to the Business world with our Advanced Consultation, Tutoring and Presentation of any Business chapter of their choice.

We "DELIVER BEYOND VALUE" no matter the size of the entity. We cater for Individuals, Public and Private Entities.

We believe in triple bottom line reporting. Honesty, Integrity and Loyalty is what we offer our clients while maintaining our Independence.

Our Primary focus is Small, Micro and Medium Entities.

MOTTO : We deliver beyond Value.
VISION : To produce entrepreneurs and/or Professional practitioners from economically disadvantaged backgrounds through providing quality services to individuals, public and private entities.

OUR MISSION STATEMENT

Corruption free and Independent
Quality Professional Service delivery
Integrity, Accountability and Transparency
Adhering to law and regulations at all times
Ethical and people centered
Empowerment of previously disadvantaged

Description of Our Services

ACCOUNTING AND BOOKKEEPING

We do personal and Business accounting. Almost all the Stakeholders make Investment and Financing decisions based on the Financial Position and Performance of an entity (Both the Income statement and the Balance sheet); this is the overall reflection of your books/business dealings in a generally accepted Accounting Practice format.
This is why they have to be prepared with great accuracy and paying attention to details, of course with necessary knowledge and according to Generally accepted accounting practices or International financial reporting standards, However, most entities often get a qualified Audit report which reflects badly on the governance and management of an entity, and this tarnish the reputation of an entity, because of costly mistakes made by in-

competent Bookkeeper or an Accountant.

Financial Statements gives stakeholders a piece of mind about the dealings of an entity, even more so since it has grown to be the rule of good governance to practice triple bottom-line reporting. Reliability and Relevance of financial statements rely on the Competency and knowledge of an Accountant/Bookkeeper. We are a team of highly capable and qualified professionals dedicated to making sure we reflect your entity as no less than it is. Sure numbers never lie, but that is only when correct measures and practices are applied.

TAXATION

Most of the Taxpayers(Both natural persons and legal entities) think they are paying way more than they should to revenue service and they probably are, However, there are legal ways to cut your Taxation liability. There are about 23 types of taxes both natural persons and legal entities are subject to, what makes matters worse is the fact that, taxation practices change every year and each require thorough understanding to apply accordingly as some are conditional. Illiteracy and/or ignorance to Law does not excuse one from Law, Often honest mistakes, misinterpretation or nondisclosures in tax calculation may in the eyes of others be seen as tax evasion, a punishable offence. Avoid penalties and tarnishing your reputation and let us do your tax numbers and you focus on running your business.

CONSULTING, TUTTORING AND PRESENTATION

By consulting, we are saying we offer in-depth knowledge, skill and expertise to your business. We give advice, solve problems, give innovative strategic ideas and make recommendations, by so doing removing uncertainties to a certain point and help you take calculated risks in whatever business decision you make.

Constant learning has become integral part of business, so as part of our consulting; we offer Tutoring and presentations on Business Chapters of your choice.

The most important Assets of any business are its employees, Invest in your business by equipping them with necessary skills and business literacy we offer with our consulting.

For example: Formulating a Business plan, Time management, Tendering, Promoting teamwork, dealing with cultural diversities in workplace, Business Ethics, etc. Every business cycle comes about with its own challenges, so with global competition and electronic market getting stronger day by day, for SMME's and Entrepreneurs, consulting has become a need for business growth and survival.

Most projects fail because most of the managers focus only on primary management tasks. We believe no issue is too small or immaterial in Business, and we are not just a team, we are a family, which is why we also as part of our Consulting are willing to even manage projects for our clients.

To most people planning your Estate seems like just your Assets consolidation, however, this is just part of the truth, with our planning; your estate runs way beyond your death, therefore are worth special management plan.

BUSINESS AGENTS/REPRESENTATIVES

Acting on Authority and client's consensus from whatever kind of contract we have, we perform any legal business act, conclude transactions and/or represent client and/or their business with expertise, skill and in-depth knowledge. We aim to deliver beyond value in whatever kind of contract we take, for our existence is worthless without the client's satisfaction.

BUSINESS/ENTREPRENEURIAL COACHING AND MENTORING

We become completely involved in your business, this is a step by step empowerment and tutoring, we become your support structure and help you grow both as an Entrepreneur and the Business, For more information about these services:

Email: Laporzito@gmail.com
Call : +2772 123 4567

MANAGEMENT INFORMATION

Last name	Moletsane
Full names	Kagiso Emmanuel
Member Interest	100%
Id Number	880816 1234 567
Marital status	Unmarried
Gender	Male
Nationality	South African
Race	African

BUSINESS QUALIFICATIONS

Qualification	Bcom (Bachelor of Commerce)
Institution	University of Limpopo
Year obtained	2009

Major Subjects : Management Accounting III

: Financial Accounting III

: Taxation III

: Auditing III

With distinctions in : Business Calculations

: Introduction to Human Resource Management

: Commercial Law

: Business Information Systems

OTHER RELEVANT QUALIFICATIONS

Certificates in : Pastel Accounting

: Project Management

: Strategic Management

: Team Leadership and Team Conflict Resolution

COMPURER SKILLS : MS Office

: Pastel Accounting

: E-Learning

THE BUSINESS PLAN

Cover page

This is the first page of a document, it tells a user what exactly is the document about without having to read/peruse through it. And it's only a sentence long; it's just saying this is a BUSINESS PLAN OF WHOEVER/WHATEVER ENTITY; just that title is enough, there is absolutely no need for bright colors, flowers or pictures, present business documents in black and white, always. Stick to basics. (especially if you do not know whom you are dealing with)

Table of contents

This is the description of what is in the document in an orderly manner the document follows. It makes it easy for a user to go directly to any chapter/heading of their choice without reading through the whole document. Numbering chapters/headings is imperative.

Executive summary and Entrepreneurial team

Paint the picture in the readers mind through words, make us see things the way you do, if this was a painting of Monalisa, then this part would be the head, this is where you give details of the founders, management skills, expertise and qualifications relevant to the business in question. This is where you sell yourself and the business. State the mission and objective of the business, its market share, reputation, history, finance needed and how the business will redeem it.

Description of business concept and the industry

Specify what is your business about, the kind of the industry a business is entering/ operating, and its volatility, give details on why you started the business? Its goal and objectives, the benefits it brings to the environment it operates within, what kind of regulations apply to the business in question? Is there a room in the market for such business to exist? What are the future plans? What is it registered with?

Market analysis

This is about knowing every detail, however material or immaterial in your market (consumers and competition), for though we may not be their servants, we serve them, you state things like;
Consumer behavioral change overtime and how you intend dealing with it with regard to the proposed business/project.

Competition

Volatility of the business
Business relationship to GDP, political landscapes, economic and business cycle
Effects of environment to business
Necessity of market segmentation
Product/service demand or demand for improved product/service
Consumer profile (knowing what are their needs and wants)
Consumer and potential consumer base
Existing and expected market share
Advertising medium/strategy and its relevance to the market
Estimated sales for a stated period

Marketing plan

This is from the making of the product, packaging, branding and to the delivering the product to the final users, how are you going to get us interested, and finally getting us in to buying whatever it is you are selling

SWOT analysis

This is the Strengths, Weaknesses, Opportunities and Threats in the business/ its environment. (Discuss each separate)
For every opportunity there is a threat, and, for every strength there is a weakness/area needing improvement. State ways you plan on turning the weaknesses in to strengths and how you are going to turn threats in to opportunities, thereby minimizing business and investment risks.

Finance plan and Budgets

Describe your financial needs and sources of finance you are planning on, is it internal (owners) or external (loans or lease)
Include projected financial statements.
The budgets must include;
Sales budget
Marketing budget
Production and procurement
Fixed costs
Cost of acquiring or renting properties
Make separate the following;
Estimated total net income
Return on investments
Estimated market share and growth
Break even
Provision for bad debts
Cash flow estimates
Business liquidity

Security
Risk management

Operation/Production plan

List your suppliers. Security and details of storage or location of operation. Labor intensive or what?
List the following;
Design and/or Floor management.
Production capacity
Address and other details of the location like its relevance, effectiveness and efficiency. Is the location owned or rented?
The cost of all the above.

Competition

What have you got that your competitor doesn't? How are you going to be able to outsmart them and enter the market they already have dominated? What can you do different that they do not? How can you add more value to the consumer than they do?

External environment risks

How does the external environment change affect the business and how can they be dealt with.
External business environment amongst others include;
The government and its agencies
Level of economic activities

Trading rules and regulations

Exchange rates
Globalization
Economic cycle
Interest rates
Legal Requirements and applicable regulations impact on busi-

ness

What are the legal requirements you have to follow/meet to enter/operate that kind of business/industry? Have you met them? What are the acts, rules and regulations applicable to only/specifically the environment/business/industry you are in?

Appendices and Business documents

Attach all the business documents like, tax registration and compliance certificate, founding documents, etc.

INTERNAL AND OPERATIONAL BUSINESS PLAN

OF RADIENT SERVANTS Cleaning Services

(For Investor sourcing and management only)

NAME OF BUSINESS	: RADIENT SERVANTS CLEANING SERVICES
BUSINESS ADRESS	: 123^B LEDUBANA SECTION BORAKALALO 2870
POSTAL ADRESS	: P O BOX 530 MOTSWEDI 2870
CONTACT PERSON	: MOLETSANE K E
CELL NUMBER	: 072 123 4567
E-MAIL ADRESS	: Laporzito@gmail.com
COMPILATION DATE	: 20 SEPTEMBER 2010

CONTENTS

1. EXECUTIVE SUMMARY

BUSINESS CONCEPT

RADINT SERVANTS cleaning service is a sole proprietorship that was formed on the 20th September 2010, with the aim of creating employment and empowering both the youth and women from previously disadvantaged backgrounds.

Our customers range from public, private, non-profit orientated businesses to individuals. We have identified an opportunity in the cleaning service industry to accomplish the entities' goal of creating employment and empowerment for the youth and women from previously disadvantaged groups.

CURRENT STATE OF BUSINESS

RADINT SERVANTS Cleaning Services is in business but has not yet started trading as customers have not yet been approached for business and funds are still to be located.

Currently the owner and founder who is now marketing the business and conducting various researches manage the business.

RADINT SERVANTS Cleaning Services is operating from the residences of the owner and storage rooms for equipment and materials will be hired at each respective place that the entity will be operating.

PRINCIPAL OWNER

Moletsane Kagiso Emmanuel
A 24 Year old male who completed his Bachelor degree in 2009 at the University of Limpopo own and runs the business solely

FINANCIAL REQUIREMENTS

NAME OF BUSINESS	: RADIENT SERVANTS CLEANING SERVICES
BUSINESS ADRESS	: 123^B LEDUBANA SECTION BORAKALALO 2870
POSTAL ADRESS	: P O BOX 530 MOTSWEDI 2870
CONTACT PERSON	: MOLETSANE K E
CELL NUMBER	: 072 123 4567
E-MAIL ADRESS	: Laporzito@gmail.com
COMPILATION DATE	: 20 SEPTEMBER 2010

2. BUSINESS DESCRIPTION

Name of business

RADINT SERVANTS cleaning services

Background

RADINT SERVANTS cleaning services is a newly formed entrepreneurial venture by Moletsane Kagiso Emmanuel as a vehicle to empower and create opportunities for youth especially previously disadvantaged, and more-so, women's.

The entity was formed after a thorough research was conducted in the cleaning services industry from which the following was concluded:

a) There are still businesses that do not hire cleaning services companies as they are perceived to be expensive,

b) The market is dominated by a few large companies.

c) There are certain businesses/groups that are overlooked by most of the cleaning services,

d) A cleaning service company is a platform for creating employment for the youth and women in the cleaning industry,

e) There is a need for affordable cleaning services.

Nature of business

RADINT SERVANTS Cleaning Services offer cleaning services on a contractual basis to specifically businesses, be it of whatever kind, both private and public. Cleaners are hired according to the needs of the customer. We also offer Once-off services for, but not limited to, after functions and flat owners, i.e. when tenants move in and/or out of flats.

Owners

RADINT SERVANTS Cleaning Services is owned solely by Moletsane Kagiso Emmanuel, a qualified Entrepreneur with, among others, Bachelors degree from University of Limpopo. The owner is passionate about job creation and youth empowerment. He is currently acting as fulltime manager of the Entity.

Location

As according to our Strategic approach to performing efficiently and effectively, Acquiring fixed property does not make financial sense in any place of our operations. The business is currently being run from the owner's respective home. As soon as we start trading, a store room-cum-office will be leased to accommodate equipment, materials and the administrative functions in every place of business we operate in.

3. DEVELOPMENT IMPACT

Through its service delivery, RADINT SERVANTS will make use of local workforce, previously disadvantaged groups around our respective areas of business
will benefit most.

5. SWOT ANALYSIS

STRENGTHS	WEAKNESSES
Marketing	**Marketing**
o We will offer affordable cleaning service and employee satisfaction leading to customer satisfaction	o As an emerging company we might not have the necessary resources to compete with established businesses
	Finance
Finance	o We offer our services on contractual basis and a lot of our working capital will be tied up in debtors
o The business is managed by youth in the financial stream of learning, so finance management will be easier.	
	Administration
Administration	o
o All the administration of the business will be done by the members who are competent and it will be cost effective.	
Human resources	
o The nature of the business does not require much in terms of management but a lot of cleaners will be employed based on demand of our services	**Human resources**
	o We will need a lot of cleaners when the business progresses and it will be difficult to keep personal contact with a lot of employees (ensuring happiness and motivation) as well as to appoint reliable employees who will not jeopardize the relationship with clients.
	Plant and equipment
Plant and equipment	o Specialized equipment will be needed for catering other clients, e.g. factories
o The business can be operated from a hired office with minimum equipment.	
o Our services are labour intensive and minimum plant is also required	
Business management	

o The business is fully managed by the founder, a well capable and qualified entrepreneur.	Business management o Though experience is just an adjustment in context and does not guarantee success, management is inexperienced
OPPORTUNITY	**THREATS**
o The industry is not fully exploited in our region; there is still room to exploit clients that are currently being overlooked by competitors. o The market is mostly dominated by few cleaning service providers; Radiant Servants will offer an alternative to unsatisfied customers and offer competition for excellent service delivery. o The business is not capital intensive and only minimum investment in cleaning equipment is made at the beginning of every contract with new customers. o Cleaning materials are readily accessible and affordable from a number of suppliers.	o As a new business we are vulnerable to established businesses, as we are not in a position to compete with them. o Because we are a new business we will not be able to gain the necessary trust from suppliers to buy materials and equipment on credit, and this has the potential to create cash flow problems o Most businesses hire their own staff for cleaning services and do not invest in cleaning services companies. o Cleaning services are regarded as an unnecessary and expensive expense by other businesses and it will be hard to get business from them.

8. MARKET OVERVIEW AND ANALYSIS

8.1. Overview and segmentation

The cleaning service industry is a labour intensive business, where services are offered to individuals and businesses personally.
The industry is categorized into three main groups : maids, janitorial and carpet and upholstery.

Maids

Maids are hired to offer cleaning services to households.

Advantage

More women are becoming career women and mostly are unable to juggle career and household chores
Disadvantage

Most people are traditional and believe a woman should do her own cleaning

janitorial

Labourers are hired by a cleaning service business to offer cleaning services to
businesses.

Advantages

Mass cleaning is possible depending on the size of the businesses
Disadvantages

Most businesses find the cleaning services expensive and hire their own staff

carpet and upholstery

Labour is hired to clean the carpets and upholstery of individuals and businesses.
This category is also capital intensive.

Advantages

Most people cannot afford to buy carpet cleaning equipment
Disadvantages

Because of the unaffordability of the carpet cleaning machinery most people do no buy carpets and upholstery.

RADINT SERVANTS cleaning services caters for all the categories that exist in the market. We have chosen to cater for all the categories as the main aim of establishing this entity was to create employment to more people who cannot help themselves.

Cleaning complexes, campuses and hospitals require a lot of labour and more people will be hired.

We also want to offer cleaning services to the small businesses that are often overlooked by cleaning service providers.

8.2. Product

Our services are categorized into two groups: contract and once off cleaning services.

Contract cleaning service

We offer cleaning service on a contract basis to businesses and government departments/offices.

Once off cleaning services

We offer cleaning services on a once off service to businesses after functions as well as to flat owners/landlords when tenants move in and out of residences.

Our main competitors are cleaning services providers who offer cleaning services to businesses on a contract basis.

We will keep abreast of competition by creating small services that are overlooked by these competitors.

We have come up with a pricing strategy that is competitive and offers value for money to the customers.

AS FORM OF EXPANSION THE FOLLOWING SERVICES ARE AMOUNGST OTHERS, UNDER EXPLORATION BY OUR RESEARCH TEAM:

Gardening services
Painting
Pest control

8.3. Price

Our price will be determined by taking the following into account:
1. Cost of labour
2. Cost of cleaning materials
3. Gross profit margin

The price will increase with every contract renewal to reflect changes in the following:
1. Cost of labour: as determined by increases in minimum wages
2. Cost of cleaning materials: as determined by inflation

8.4. Promotion

The entity will offer a discount to contract clients on any one month of their choice. This however will apply to clients that pay on a monthly basis.
Tissues and refuse bags will be given to clients who do not use them on a large scale e.g. offices and shops. This will however be included as part of contract price to other clients.

8.5. Distribution

As a service business, RADINT SERVANTS will provide cleaning services to clients at their premises and no middlemen is needed. Clients will be approached and cleaning proposals made directly by management.

8.6. Customer analysis

Our customers comprises of different businesses:
Complexes
Shops
Universities, technikons, colleges
Private school
Hospitals
Police stations
Flat owners
Municipalities
Stadiums(after functions)
Office buildings(including government offices)
Our A-list customers will be:
hospitals
municipalities
complexes
They are our A-list customers because
these customer groups will enable us to reach our goal of creating
employment as they require mass cleaning
they will also represent a large portion of our revenue
they are also profitable

8.7. Competitive advantages

To be competitive we have identified customers that are not serviced by most cleaning service companies, this include:
Flat owners
Small shops
We have created a formula for calculating our service price, which will ensure that customers pay accordingly for the service they receive and the business will make a reasonable profit with every engagement

8.8. Competitive advantages

Most of the cleaning companies employed in Northwest are from other provinces and we want to convince clients to make use of local services as a means to create employment and promote triple bottom line while looking after their stakeholders

Existing cleaning service entities charge higher prices for their services which discourage other potential clients to make use of cleaning services.

6. CRITICAL SUCCESS FACTORS (projections)

Key area of business	Critical factors
Marketing	Market share By the end of our first year we want to have 5 contract clients Gross margins Our targeted gross profit margin is 30% Our targeted net profit margin is 15%
Human resources	Management Management is the responsibility of the members Personnel At least 20 cleaners will be on our database and payroll for contract and casual employees by end of first year.

7. OWNER AND MANAGEMENT INFO

7.1. Owner and Manager

Last name	Moletsane
Full names	Kagiso Emmanuel
Member Interest	100%
Id Number	880816 1234 567
Marital status	Unmarried
Gender	Male
Nationality	South African
Race	African

BUSINESS QUALIFICATIONS

Qualification	Bcom (Bachelor of Commerce)
Institution	University of Limpopo
Year obtained	2009

Major Subjects   : Management Accounting III

: Financial Accounting III

: Taxation III

: Auditing III

With distinctions in   : Business Calculations

: Introduction to Human Resource Management

: Commercial Law

: Business Information Systems

OTHER RELEVANT QUALIFICATIONS

Certificates in   : Pastel Accounting

: Project Management

: Strategic Management

: Team Leadership and Team Conflict Resolution

COMPURER SKILLS   : MS Office

: Pastel Accounting

: E-Learning

A market related salary will be awarded based on contribution to the day-to-day running of the business.

9. TECHNICAL REVIEWS

9.1. Production process (service process)

The cleaning service will be provided at the client's premises by cleaning staff recruited by RADINT SERVANTS.
The number of cleaners will be determined by the size of the client's premises
Experienced and inexperienced cleaners will be considered and mixed so they can learn from each other
Working days of cleaners will be determined by working days of the client, normally 5-6 days a week, but the hours will be determined accordingly and in accordance with Labor Act.

9.2. Location and premises

RADINT SERVANTS does not own any premises but plans are made to lease an office-cum-storeroom in each location we will operate.
This office will be used for administration of the business and for storing unused equipment and cleaning chemicals (of Corse care will be taken and all the necessary risk measures).
Leasing will be cost effective as Radiant Servants does not require fixed property.

9.3. Machinery

The industry is labor intensive and does not require the use of machinery. However, cleaning equipment are required, the nature of which will be determined by the cleaning requirements of clients, e.g. offices vs. complexes vs. factories

9.4. Insurance

RADINT SERVANTS will not own premises or any specialized machinery and our insurable risks are minimal at most environments if not absent.

9.5. Legality and regulatory

As a labour intensive business Radiant Servants will employ a large number of cleaners.
As such we are compelled by law to register all our employees with the unemployment insurance fund.
Radiant Servants also has to take into accounts such issues as workman compensation act and other labour safety requirements.
We also have to adhere to the minimum wages act, and BEE as laid out by the department of labour.

9.6. Management information systems

Management will make use of a personal computer to record the accounting entries of the business as well as keep a database of labour and suppliers as well as customers. Necessary Softwares (e.g. pastel) will be purchased to ensure audit trail and the safety of documents and accounting records and to minimize unauthorized access to management accounts.

9.8. Raw materials

Cleaning chemicals are readily accessible from local chemical suppliers around town and a number of potential suppliers have been identified. Payment terms will be negotiated with suppliers, where applicable to ensure that the corporation does not encounter cash flow problems.

9.9. Labour

RADINT SERVANTS will employ labour depending on the requirements of clients. Labour will be classified under long term and temporary. Long term will represent labour that will work for contract clients and the term of employment will be determined by the duration of contract between basomi and its clients. Temporary/casual labour will be labour that will work for once off engagements such as cleaning flats when tenants move in/out, however their contacts will be saved on basomi database to be contacted for further engagements

10. FINANCIAL REVIEW

10.1. Source of funds

Working capital will be needed to start operating the business, for the first few months. Loans will be applied for from organizations that offer funding to businesses (no bank loans).The loan needed will be repaid within 12-18 months. RADINT SERVANTS is a new business, which does not own assets and therefore does not have the security for the loan thereof.

4. FINANCIAL REQUIREMENTS

Total funds required   12184

To be applied as follows (Operational)

Cleaning equipment	5325
Cleaning chemicals	2878
Cleaning materials	2735
Uniforms	1246
Marketing expenses	

10.2. Application of funds

The funds will be used to finance the following items

CLEANING EQUIPMENT			
Description	Units	Unit price(R)	Total (R)
Single bucket trolley	5	415	2075
Double bucket trolley	5	650	3250
			5325
CLEANING MATERIALS			
Large mops	10	48	480
Broom	10	42	420
Long handle dustpan set	10	50	500
Toilet brush	10	29	290
Refuse bags(100s)black	2	60	120
Toilet papers(48s)	5	125	625
Small buckets(5l)	10	10	100
Mutton cloth(500g)	10	20	200
			2735
CLEANING CHEMICALS			
Furniture polish(1l)	10	24	240
Floor stripper(25l)	1	256	256
Handy cleaner(25l)	2	180	360
Multipurpose cleaner(25l)	2	185	370
Pine gel(25l)	2	256	512
Super shine(25l)	2	300	600
Toilet bowl cleaner(25l)	1	155	155
Universal cleaner(25l)	1	185	185
Window cleaner(25l)	1	200	200

			2878
UNIFORMS			
Ladies uniforms	7	77.29	541
Men's trousers	3	69.99	210
Men's jackets	3	65	195
Men's t-shirts	3	42	126
Printing	10		174
			1246
GRAND TOTAL			12184

This budget was prepared on an assumption of a contract/s that requires 10 employees and that all equipment and materials will be divided equally among the cleaners.

10.3. Financial projections

RADINT SERVANTS Cleaning Services does not have any historic financial data or past trading that can be used to make any financial projections.

STRATEGIC PLAN (MANAGEMENT) (INTERNAL)

PHASE 1 (to be completed by end of 2019)

PINACLE VIEW TOURS AND EVENTS SPECIALISTS

INTRODUCTION

We are a team of travel influencers and events specialists, offering the most exclusive and elite intra south-african experience, specially adapted and personalised tourism packages suited for client's lifestyle, compiled as per client's individual needs and specifications with both the budget and time in considerations, yet as professional and classy as it gets. We pride ourselves in understanding and acknowledging the fact that no two clients are the same, hence we focus on tailor-made and unique service offerings.

We offer breath taking and diverse views of our country as original and pure as it is, be it a retreat, exploration, merely to experience different ways of life, or to create priceless and everlasting memories, we are the go to guys.

We cater for both local and international clients.

OUR SPECIALITY

We have classified our market in to three classes:

Individuals

Adventure trips
Honey moon packages
Spa getaways
Hotel bookings
Wedding celebrations
Party organising
Event design and deco
Luxury holidays
Family vacations
Bae-cations

Businesses and NPO's

Bookings (accommodation and flights)
Closing and farewell parties
Incentive getaways
Networking events
Conference organising

Schools

Bosberaad
Matric Dance and ball
Accommodation and transportation bookings
Field trips
OUR SUPPLIERS AND TRAVEL PATNERS

Depending on the nature of a project and the location thereof, we work with highly rated, recognised and certified local service providers who have distinguished themselves with the focus being on empowering the locals and high standard of ethicality. We have above standard vetting methodology on choosing our suppliers and travel partners.
PRIMARY MARKETING, OPERATIONAL AND PR TOOLS

Since the focus is on influencing and dominating the current market, our niche is socially and economically active market
We have identified the following ways as a way to market ourselves:
Social Media (as a primary platform for influencing and leading)

90% of our target market is active on social media, hence this is our primary marketing tool. Due to the stigmatisation of travelling associated with the wealthy and of no valuable purpose, we will use our social media platforms as a way to educate about travelling and the history of our places as a way to lure and influence our potential clients on our different types of travel and events offerings.
This will also serve as a way to know if we are on point or not since its public and therefore any review on our services will be noted and so is our reaction to this.

Public functions

By this we mean we will attend public functions and be a part of them one way or another, we will either sponsor the event or be a part of the speakers and thereby market our services

Business networking groups

Networking with other professionals and likeminded individuals from different spheres of the business will reveal if any the opportunities we might be able to capitalise on, what we can do better and what we are currently excelling on since we aim on delivering the best service possible.

Youth sports programmes (make travel and exploration a passion for youth)

Sports bar and restaurant (also as travel partners)

Travel pop up parties(party on the road)

SWOT ANALYSIS

STRENGTH

Diversified client base
Combination of skills on employees(highly trained and skills)
Extensive advertising and marketing

WEAKNESSES

New team members who is yet to learn each other's skills and expertise
Lack of reputation in relation to our competitors
Lack of strategic allies
Dependence on other service provides

OPPORTUNITIES

Government drive in terms of BEE
Current growth in the industtry

THREATS

Established tourism destination are creating their inhouse services
Existing competition
Little profit margin

NECESSARY TOOLS
High resolution drone
Laptop

Cell phone
High resolution cam
Moderm and portable wifi connector
Cam stand

NICHE COMPOSITION
INDIVIDUALS (to and from)
Zeerust to Durban
Zeerust to Cape town
Zeerust to Suncity
Zeerust to Belabela
Zeerust to Haartebees
Zeerust to Mafikeng (60's, mahika a mahikeng, incl mmabatho palms)

Intra cruising (Zeerust to Suncity to Belabela to Haartebees to mmabatho palms)
Coast to coast cruising (Zeerust to Suncity, to Haartebees, to Durban, to Cape Town

EVENTS TO PLAN AROUND (CAPE-TOWN)

CONFIRMATION	DATE HAPPENING	LOCATION/EVENT
CONFIRMED	End 31 March	Kristenbosch Summer concerts
CONFIRMED CONFIRMED	End 28 Feb	Stellenbosch Street Soirees
	End 31 March	Open Streets
CONFIRMED	End 31 March	Live @ Vergenoegd Low
CONFIRMED	End 31 March	Concerts in the park
CONFIRMED	26 to 28 April	SA Cheese festival
CONFIRMED	29 April to 5 May	Afrikaburn
CONFIRMED	1 to 5 May	Decorex
CONFIRMED	17 to 19 May	Franschoek Literary Festival
CONFIRMED	7 to 17 june	Hermanus FynArts
CONFIRMED	27 June to 7 July	National Arts Festival
CONFIRMED	29 Aug to 1 Sep	Homemakers Expo
CONFIRMED	18 to 27 October	Open Design Festival

Cape Town Standard Package
Includes:
A flight From Johannesburg International Airport to Cape town international airport and return
Accomodation includes, Protea Presidential Hotel
Free breakfast
Aiport shuttle
Spa services
Gym
Air conditioning and standard room services

It's a 4 days 3 nights trip. From Thursday afternoon to Sunday morning

Accommodation (2 Adults Sharing)	10000
Flight prices	2500
Cab to airport (to/from zeerust)	1000
TOTAL TRIP FARES (2 PPL)	R13500

Payments Options

DURATION	PAYMENT	TOTAL
9 Months	1600 (800 Each)	13500 (6750 Each)
6 Months	2250 (1125 Each)	13500 (6750 Each)
4 Months	3375 (1688 Each)	13500 (6750 Each)
3 Months	4500 (2250 Each)	13500 (6750 Each)

To keep price attractive and competitive, we do not add profit margin, the profit will be the discount we receive from booking both the accommodation and transportation, it is usually 10% of the normal price per room.
MARKETING EXPENSES BUDGET
Advertising:
Printed material
Online material

Radio and tv ads
Ad company
Other

TOTAL Sales and marketing expenses
Percentage of sales

You already know this is just an example, the point here is the format not the numbers, hence I will not be including them.

SALES FORECAST

SALES	YEAR 1	YEAR 2	YEAR 3
All tourist services			
other			
TOTAL SALES			
COST OF SALES	YEAR1	YEAR 2	YEAR 3
All tourist services			
Other			
TOTAL COST OF SALES			

PERSONNEL EXPENDITURE PLAN

	YEAR 1	YEAR 2	YEAR 3
Directors			
Accountant			
Tour guide			
Sales and marketing			
Driver			
Cleaner			
Security			

GENERAL ASSUMPTIONS

	YEAR 1	YEAR 2	YEAR 3
Current interest			
Long term interest			
Tax rate			
other			

PRO FORMA PROFIT AND LOSS

	YEAR 1	YEAR 2	YEAR 3
Sales			
Cost of sales			
Other			
Total COS			
Gross margin			
Gross margin %			
EXPENSES			
Payroll			
Sales and marketing			
Depreciation			
Stationery			
Data and airtime			
electricity			
Leased equipment			
Office Rent			

Miscellaneous			
Travel			
Insurance			
Maintenance			
TOTAL EXPENSES			
PROFIT BEFORE TAX			
CURRENT TAX			
NETT PROFIT			

PROFOMA CASH FLOW

	YEAR 1	YEAR 2	YEAR 3
Cash received			
Cash from operations			
Cash from receivables			
SUBTOTAL FROM OPERATIONS			
Additional cash received			
Sales tax/vat received			
New current borrowing			
New current liabilities			
New non-current liabilities			
Sales of current assets			
Sales of long term assets			
New investment received			
SUBTOTAL CASH RECEIVED			
Expenditures			
Expenditure from operations			
Cash spending			
Bill payments			
SUBTOTAL SPENT ON OPERATIONS			
Additional spent			
Sales tax/vat			
Principal repayment of current borrowing			
Noncurrent liability repayments			
Other liability repayments			
Purchas other current assets			

Purchase of non-current assets			
Dividends			
SUBTOTAL CASH SPENT			
NETT CASH FLOW			
CASH BALANCE			

PROJECTED BALANCE SHEET

	YEAR1	YEAR 2	YEAR3
Assets (closing balance)			
Current balance (Assets)			
Current assets			
Cash			
Receivables			
Inventory			
Other current assets			
TOTAL C.A			
NON-CURRENT ASSETS			
PPE			
TOTAL ASSETS			
Current liabilities			
Payables			
Current borrowings			
Other current liabilities			
SUBTOTAL C.L			
Non-current liabilities			
TOTAL LIABILITIES			
PAID IN CAPITAL			
RETAINED EARNINGS			
EARNINGS			
NET WORTH			

PART 3

ENTREPRENEURIAL ROUTE

WHAT TO CONSIDER WHEN CHOOSING A TYPE OF BUNSIESS (ENTREPRENEURIAL ROUTE)

Amongst others;
Nature of investment/capital needed or available
Risk exposure
Nature of responsibility
Nature of obligation
Legal personality of the business
Tax structures and benefits
Number of shareholder limitation
Type of ownership
Business Industry/ Environment
Expected Return
Authority vested in the owner
Laws and regulations (Registration and procedures)

TYPES OF BUSINESS VENTURES (THE MOST COMMON)
SOLE PROPRIETOR

Commonly referred to a one men business, the following are facts about sole proprietorship, amongst others;
Easy to start and/or close
All income is the owners
Owner responsible for losses

Owner is responsible for the organizational management functions

It ceases to exist if sold, at owner's death, or owner is incapacitated to run it

Financing capacity and credit worthiness is limited to the owner's assets

Taxed on owner's income.

PARTNERSHIP

The following are facts about partnership, amongst others;
Partners are between 2 and 20
Each member contribute towards the starting capital
Profit sharing is between all partners
Taxed on the hands of each member, not jointly
Not easy to find suitable partner
Each partner is authorized to make any management decision
Dissolved in any kind of membership composition
Difficult for a partner to withdraw from it as it affects the whole business
Owners are jointly liable for debts

CLOSE CO-OPERATION

The following are facts about a close co operation, amongst others;
No shareholders only members
Members are between 1 and 10
Only natural persons can form a close co-operation
The trading name has to be registered and the name end with the abbreviation CC
The registered name, number and members names must appear on all business documents
Members have limited liability
Must have a founding statement
Simple decision making structure and decisions can be made in-

formally

All members are a part of management

It has a legal personality and therefore pays its own tax and have limitless lifetime

Auditing is not compulsory, it's a management decision, only an accounting officer is required

Its objectives or mission can be changed/added/reduced by just registering them

Due to member restriction and limited liability it's hard to secure finance

Other members consent is needed if any of them want to sell interests

PRIVATE COMPANY

The following are facts about a private company, amongst others;

Shareholders between 1 and 50

Pty (ltd) is always at the end of the private company's name.

Taxed independently from owners

It's a legal requirement to have an auditor

Have to be registered with the companies' registrar

Shareholder limited liability

Obliged to have annual general meetings

It has a legal personality

Free and easy share transferability

Memorandum of association and articles of association is needed to form this.

Must meet extra costs.ie registration costs

Extensive procedures for appointing managers

The company's business is public knowledge

THE BASICS

Mismanaging time is like telling a lie, to substantiate it; you have to tell another lie, meaning you simply have to waste another time to recover the time you have already wasted.

More likely than not, it is true that the only thief of time is procrastination. The first step to effective and efficient time management is to have power over one's life. Having power over one's life is having power over time, this is the only way as time can never be saved/stopped, once it is lost it can never be recovered.

Money and oxygen may seem like the most important things in life, but without time, they are as good as none existant.

Time is life, and time management can only be achieved through self/personal management. Time management teaches one to be;

More responsible

Accountable

Confident in their work

Time cautious (never missing a deadline)

Aware of one's Strength and areas of improvement

Self motivation and increased personal performance

More professional, and always ready for a challenge.

Reduce stress, rage and public outburst

It has become evident that in business, the ability of a man who has nothing, to add value to the entity is assessed and measured by how well he/she manage his/her own life. Ability to manage one's own life is a sign of maturity and responsibility. Coping with pressure in one's own life show that you can work with and possibly manage people, it shows you have discipline. Bad self management means bad professional management and possibly unethical behavior, and can even lead to health problems.

Self management teaches values and attitude that allow one to use one's own judgement and act on one's feet. Timing is everything in business, you snooze you loose.

Above all, responsibility is time's worst enemy. E.g. the after effect of heavy drinking is a headache in the morning which will cost another countless things.

The wait and see approach will get you nowhere, it is laziness at its best, nothing will come to you, go and get it. Just like you never stop aging, time does not stop ticking and toking either, make most of what you have, i.e. while waiting for your meeting to start, you can go through your mails or surf the net for something you might need later. Use your gadgets to your advantage, diary is never old-fashioned, it simply organize your details timely.

If you want to be the president, that's great, but how are you going to get there should really be what matters, you should break it in to step by step project, starting with the step you are taking NOW!!! Have a daily, weekly and monthly progress check, otherwise how are you ever going to know if you are getting closer to the set goal and/being effective?

Avoid contingency situations, they mess with your time, if it's not in your plan to have dinner with your co-workers, then do not have dinner with them, do what you have planned to do by then.

Centre your life around you, not your job or your life partner. Skip a difficult task and get to it later, why bother waste time on something you probably don't have clue about?

Leaders waste their time checking on delegated tasks, you delegated that task to that specific person for a reason, you trust him/her, I'm all for perfectionists but imagine how your delegate's morale is going to be when you go through everything he/she did, if you are going to go through it, why not do it yourself? You should be focused on the end results, if it's done then great, it does not matter who did it, and hence business is a team sport.

Set goals must be Realistic

They must be time and cost measurable

They must meet the resources available to achieve them.

In conclusion, procrastination is more or less like masturbation, you are messing with yourself.

Need to know basis

An entrepreneur does not just divulge information or what he reckons to be an opportunity anywhere with anyone. Be selective when discussing your business dealings, though the world is big enough for every Entrepreneur to make money, people can easily profit from your idea while you are still beating around the bush. Always remember your competition, just like you, they do not want to be left behind, and they will do anything to be a step ahead of everyone in the game and be the customer's favourite, thereby eliminating the competition. I am not saying launch a War against the competition, I am saying not everyone plays by the book, so watch your back and always protect your interests.

Socialization and Networking (Life beyond Business)

Business life is much easier when you are everyone's friend. Attend business seminars. Reach out and lend a hand where and when you can, give favours and when you need one yourself, it won't be difficult to ask. But choose who you deal with carefully for any action of the person you are associated with will be directly/indirectly reflected on you, your reputation and your business.

Distance yourself from people dealing illegally and/or unethical as this will ruin you too, be it a family member, friend or mentor, it is not good for business.

Eyes and Ears on the streets (social media, streets know no lie)

Know what is up. Timing is everything in business. Know what your consumers want, what excites them and what doesn't, people's behaviour changes with times, and so does our needs and wants. Therefore one must always know what is HOT and NOT, be part of the society you serve, know them, what they are thinking, and where their lifestyle is heading.

Competitor acknowledgement

Your competitors are not your enemies, if a project is too big for one entity to handle, invite them in and team up, no man is an Island, and besides, this is not about you, it's about giving your customers an experience to remember, superior quality and value for money product, and of course the both of you making money along the way and enhancing your reputation to secure your long term survival.

Patience

You are not going to be rich today or tomorrow, as it has been said, easy come easy go. Patience is a virtue. Hang in there, but not with your hands folded together, hang in there with your teeth clenched on business, with sweat, blood, and tears. You will somehow or somewhere fail to achieve what you wanted to accomplish, maybe you will get a part thereof or nothing, and more likely if you worked hard, you will get there later than you had planned, but this does not matter, what matters is how you will rise after that, how you will finally get what you were after, contrary to popular beliefs, it is not about the journey to the destination, it is about the destination.

Your plans will be derailed on the way, but only you can ensure you get there, timeously or otherwise. Most of the successful entrepreneurs are those whom have done it numerous times before finally being credited for it.

External consultant and/or evaluator

External opinion on the operations of the business and how you can reduce your costs/produce more effectively worth your limited resources will go a long way.
The fact that you are making money and your customers are sat-

isfied, or you have the best peoples for the job, does not mean there is no room for improvement, there will always be a room for improvement, there is no perfect business model, or one that last over time.

Most entrepreneurs have the impression that an external consultant is only necessary when they are in trouble, they are wrong, you have to know how other experts see your business and its potential if not current weaknesses/risks. A perspective of a third party, you cannot possibly be the only expert alive.

The name

Reputation and perception is everything in business, live with the rules, be the brand you business is trying to portray. Live your profession. You cannot succeed as a business professional if you are going to be unethical or be a bad influence to those around you. It is this very people that make you and your business. As an entrepreneur, be someone to be aspired and reckoned with, lead by example, and whatever the challenge, keep your composure and never let your guard down. People are watching, and whatever you do, it will reflect not just on you, but on your business, your career and equally to those associated with you.

Constant learning

Diversifying your skills as an entrepreneur is a must lately, change has become the only certain thing in business. You have to learn to adapt, embrace and use these changes to your advantage. With every challenge comes an opportunity. You have to be ready for whatever life/business environment throws at you. You can be sure there will be no time to stop, then go and learn quickly, by the time you are done, there will be something new to and different to deal with, be proactive and deal with it before it deals with you

Good corporate governance

This means making it an organizational culture to adhere and aspiring to be the greatest in achieving the highest standards of professionalism. To pride yourself in doing what is right, to lead by example, To put people first. Looking after anything and everyone that is part of, may be, and is around and/or affected by your business both directly and/or indirectly, for without it/them, there will be no you and/or the promise for a better tomorrow.

Hard Work

Most Entrepreneurs often say the secret to success is hard work, this couldn't be more truer. Hard work does not mean digging fountains or moving mountains with your bare hands, it means giving whatever you do your all, utilizing recourses available to you effectively and efficiently to their full potential and to achieve more than what an ordinary person would have done, it means putting in extra hours, skills, being innovative and more learning. Being disciplined and loyal to yourself on being your own boss.

Loyalty

It seems as if this is the rare commodity to acquire nowadays, be loyal to yourself, those around you and mostly, those who made you. Betrayal is a very hard thing to swallow in business, no man is an island, you will need someone someday, so be loyal to everyone but never under any circumstance be unethical or be loyal to someone doing unethical/illegal thing, in fact distance yourself as far as possible from the person in question.

Time Management

Organizing you schedule timeously, knowing when to do what, and when to be where whenever will make your life easier as an

Entreprenuer. Most entrepreneurs find their gadgets to be indispensable for this reason. Loosing time is losing money, every second counts, so manage your time so it suits you personal life and it makes your work easy and effective as an Entrepreneur.

Synergy

1 + 1 = 4.
This means if we all work together towards the same goal we can achieve more than what we would have should we have rode individually. Accepting one's limits and being man enough to recognize you need the other's skill and expertise to further your goals. You cannot be an expert in all the areas of business. Some are experts in some areas, if you work your part and others work theirs according to our expertise, then what we will achieve will be a dream people often term perfection.

Calculated risks

Taking risk is a good thing, only if you are aware and have devised a plan or a counter attack of/for that risk.

Attention to details

It is the little thing that matters the most, And this is not just in terms of reporting, we are talking all round I.e. serving complimentary tea to a customers during a cold day while he/she came shopping.

Gadgets (Quick contacts)

Technological awareness, access to such, and knowing how to use them effectively, efficiently and to your advantage.

Priority

Being self disciplined to be able to prioritize and sticking to your priority.

Just in time delivery

Time is money, not just your time, every ones, so receive and deliver in time.

Change is a necessary evil; it is the master that comes about with Disruption of the norm, which may often seem as challenging our very believe systems, professionalism, ethicality and at times principles.
It is the new world order, With change come curiosity, uncertainties, growth, risk, challenges, fear, Empowerment and a chance to explore new possibilities and opportunities depending on one's view.
However great or minimal, it is enough to make even the greatest jump ship

In any business, be it a goods or service provider, you are essentially selling something, it doesn't matter if you source it from elsewhere or manufacture it yourself, therefore there are bound to be some expectations regarding you or your business and whoever is consuming your product. If you are providing some goods or service to any business or you are sourcing something from someone/some business there are bound to be some expectations regarding the viability amongst other things regarding the product in question. All the above can be put into a simple term called a contract. You enter into a contract with a certain entity or business to receive or provide a product agreed upon by the both of you as per the requirements defined by both parties.

CONTRACTS

A contract is recognised by law and it can either be verbal or written so long as it meets certain requirements although we suggest everything should be in writing for audit trail and reference. If a contract does not meet the following requirements, it cannot be recognised as a valid contract in the eyes of the law, such requirements are:

Consensus- simply put this means both parties to the contract must be in agreement and have solid intentions of making whatever they agree on possible.

Contractual capacity- both the parties entering in to a contract must have necessary capacity as recognised by law, for example, one cannot enter in to a contract with a minor or a person with mental illness.

Physical possibility- the performance or delivery of either the service or goods agreed upon by the parties must be realistic and physically possible or can at least be expected to be by the time both parties enter in to a contract

Lawfulness- this is exactly what it sounds like, you cannot enter in to an agreement that's debatable or that's opposing the law, the contract should be legal and contain legal thing.

Formalities- the contract should be as per regulation and rules contained in the law, it should be as accepted by both the business and legal community.

CODE OF CONDUCT

A code of conduct is set of rules and regulation composed with the aim of promoting fairness and equal rights to a certain group of individuals that spend some time together for or towards a common course. It guides their moral and professional behavior, it addresses the issues of diversity, be it a cultural, professional or a moral believe. It must be adhered to by each and every one, and the consequence of its breach applies not just fairly but equal to any member of that specific group regardless of their caliber or social standing, none is above it. It must be in line with the national constitution and not challenge or be against any rule of law. The following are some basic guidelines:

OBJECTIVITY AND INTEGRITY

This means being fair, open and honest, having strong moral system and being independent from any kind of influence that may cloud you judgment/decision making.

PROFFESIONAL STANDARDS

This means meeting professional requirements and standards, being competent, armed with skill, knowledge and information to make you confident on what you do.

PROFFESIONAL BEHAVIOUR

This is being a professional, leading as an example in the discipline/ environment or the Entity. It's more like being an ambassador of what you do and where you do it. It's your conduct in and out of your workplace. It promotes professionalism, discipline and Responsibility.

EQUALITY

It offers every one equal rights and benefits. Everyone must be treated with fairness, courtesy and consideration.

OPENNESS AND TRANSPARENCY

Fair trial, openness and transparency must be the golden rule. Everyone must be afforded the right to have a say and be heard and considered. In case of mistakes being made, this must be communicated to the affected party and he/she must be remedied in a fair and just way that do not put him/her in a state less than what he/she was in.

BUSINESS/ CORPORATE GOVERNANCE

What is corporate governance?

The way in which a business is conducted, operated, directed and controlled.

What are the benefits Of good corporate governance?

Sustainable Growth - business survival over time and assumption of going concern is highly probable when the business has good corporate governance structures and/or controls.

Long term risk management- Good corporate governance structures help manage risks way over business operations that may harm the survival and/or reputation of the business over a long term

Investor confidence - investors, locally or offshore, prefer a business with good corporate governance structures any day, and will even pay premium to acquire a piece of it at any given day.

Social Power(street credibility) - business outreach is more powerful than any organization/movement, for example, creating job for just 1 person will probably benefit more than 5 people in a lot of ways, i.e. their health insurance, basic needs, and status. Business is therefore seen as a number one community supporter/ builder wherever it operates.

Shareholder activism -shareholders have faith in a business with good corporate governance structures, and this may lead to long-term investments, financing and the likes

Characteristics of good corporate governance

Discipline - this means making it your way of life to constantly behave in a way that is acceptable to society, adhere to legal, cultural or any kind of rules while in and out of business environment.

Accountability -Being liable, full responsible and ready to answer to any stakeholder of the business your actions and/or decisions.

Transparency -make available for analysis, judgement and interpretation the information which represent a true reflection of the operations of the entity to the stakeholders in time

Fairness -Having equal consideration to the needs of the stakeholders, acknowledging and respecting the rights of various groups equally and without prejudice.

Independence - mental independence to avoid bias, conflict & potential conflict of interest and clouded judgements no matter the kind of relationship you have with a stakeholder/whoever in question.

Responsibility -One is responsible towards all stakeholders of the business, he/she must have behavior that allows for taking the right measures/decision when in a certain position or environment with knowledge and willingness to bear the consequences.

Social Responsibility -Taking in to account, working with, and supporting each and every stakeholder and the environment you function within, being aware of their needs, issues and challenges, and helping them make their lives better with strict consideration of your ethical conduct over a long term.

INVESTING AND FINANCING IN A BUSINESS

Becoming a successful Entrepreneur does not necessary mean you have to become a business guru, come up with a billion dollar idea or have something special. We have to acknowledge the fact that we can't all be cut out to be business sharks, but we can all be in business if we so deem. Investing and/or Financing a business idea/operation is another of many ways a person can be involved or even own a business without having to take the traditional route.

Investing in a business means putting money, or something relevant to the success of business of which its value can be measured in terms of money and the value thereof is certain, in a business, in return for a part thereof or a specified potion of the profits it will/ is estimated to make until it is dissolved or the investor change his investing decision unless otherwise agreed. Investing in a business entitles the investor a certain amount of shares in the business. However, there are different classes of shares in the business and are so classified according to risks an investor is willing to take in investing in a business, these are: Ordinary shares, which are often available to investors without any contact or negotiation between the company and the investor, they are obtainable from Johannesburg Stock Exchange, and only a registered broker can buy shares on behalf of an investor, meaning you have to find a competent broker to obtain shares from the stock exchange. Stock brokers do not only buy shares on behalf of investors, they also manage these shares, on the investors consent of course, and the investor's decision is final. The Ordinary shares are the most risky shares there is, and the return thereof is not guaranteed. By obtaining shares, it gives the investor the right to dividends (share in declared profits) and share growth (increase in share growth)

Period of return or profit split is never guaranteed. And Preference shares, these shares are more secured and less risky, they can be redeemed by the business whenever they deem so as they are conditional. The returns are guaranteed. Investor does not get involved in the daily running of the business, he/she does not at all have a say in the business except if what he/she own is more than half of the business, or is a majority shareholder which makes him/her a majority shareholder. Debentures, this is a loan to the company, the investment and its interest is guaranteed, it is the most secured thing close to the Government bonds, these loans however have special conditions attached to them by both the lender and the business in most instances, it is limited by time. Government bonds, these are the safest form of investment, it means you borrow the government money and they guarantee you a certain amount of return for a certain amount of time, and as you can imagine how difficult it is for a government to be broke, it is the reason they are the safest, and low return as they are almost risk free financial instruments.

Investing in business through financial means is not the only way to invest, one can contribute anything that is relevant to the success of a business, both tangible and intangible, for example, a contributing a skill is an investment, and/or contributing a car, computer, etc is also an investment.

Financing a business idea/ a business in general is more like you are making a loan to the business. You put in your money with the knowledge of how much you are going to be paid, how much, and how long it will take before you are paid your money and the interest thereof. When you finance a business, you do not get any type of ownership in a business, reviewing business operations may at times be permitted even though it has to be disclosed before the investor enter in to a contract with a business. The return on the investor's money is guaranteed, and should the business collapse, the investor enjoys preference to be paid over any other shareholders. The return normally does not depend on the success of a project or business, and only interest on the finance

acquired is payable to the investor, no dividends.
Investing does not only have to be money, it can also be a skill
and/or experience.

LOWERING INVESTMENT AND/OR FINANCING RISK

The most effective way of ensuring income and lowering the risk
is to diversify. The say do not put all your eggs in one basket apply.
If for example you invest in a cold drink and a coffee, it will be
a great diversification move; the reason being the cold drink will
bring in more income in summer and less in winter, and the opposite will apply in relation to coffee as it is consumed more in
winter and less in summer. From the above example we can conclude that the investor will on average get more or less the same
amount of re return every season. A bad investment move will be
to invest in say cows and butchery, if the cows are dead or ill the
butchery can't make up for that as it is dependent on cows.
Investment/ financing risk can be minimized in a lot of ways. For
example, it is clear that investing in a well-known and successful
company is less risky than investing in a none-existing or a devel-
oping entity. One way of averting risk will be to check the moral
status of the entity, social responsibility and corporate government of the business. For example, a global warming cautious
company is less risky than a company that simply does not care
about carbon emission they produce or its surrounding as the
latter has greater chances of suffering reputational damage and
countless environmental damage claims in future.
Diversifying means bringing different investments (as much and
as different as possible) in to your investment bucket to ensure
constant inflow of returns and avert investment risks.

DO'S

Be confident and never drop your guard

Plan and be proactive
Keep learning
Take calculated risks
Have mental independence
Inspire, motivate and help where you can
Listen and respect everyone
Obey your rules
Follow the golden rule (do unto others as you would like others to do unto you)
Be Specific, Manager (business leader), Ambitious, Reliable, and Time cautious

DON'T

Take short cuts
Stop learning
Risk more than you can afford to loose
Procrastinate
Make exceptions
Let your confidence slip
Be over confident
Break promises and/or make one's you cannot keep
Judge people
Be greedy

ABOUT THE AUTHOR

Kagiso Emmanuel Moletsane

Mr Moletsane is a Bcom graduate from the University of Limpopo(RSA), with distinctions in Introduction to Human Resourse, Commercial Law, Business information systems and Business calculations. Certificates in Project management, Strategic management, conflict resolution & team leadership and pastel accounting.

He started his proffesion as a Financial accountant at a Sherrif's office, from which after realising the need for financiall literacy, He worked as a Senior Financial consultant both locally(RSA) and International consulting with over 5000 individuals. With realisation that most engage in wastefull and irresponsible spending habits in their youth only to learn way too late in life, He went on to become a high school business teacher in RSA. Currently he is dedicated to reaching the masses through writting financial literacy books and only consult on occation as he firmly believe financial freedom is a choice.